TENDER OF WISHES

FOR MY PARENTS

THE PRAYERS OF A YOUNG PRIEST

JAMES
CARROLL

NEWMAN PRESS
PARAMUS, N.J. : NEW YORK, N.Y.
TORONTO : LONDON

Designed and illustrated by Emil Antonucci

Cover photo by Fortune Monte

Library of Congress
Catalog Card Number: 73-92219

Published by Newman Press
Editorial Office: 304 West 58 Street, N. Y. 10019
Business Office: Paramus, New Jersey 07652

Printed and bound in the
United States of America

TENDER OF WISHES

CONTENTS

"We do not know how to pray as we ought . . ."
Romans 8,26

The early ones of us, O Lord,
asked you how to pray.
You answered only with your life
saying nothing about the what
or how of effective words.
You conducted no workshops,
gave no formulas,
but only one sign,
the sign of Jonas and others
who came to terms with God
and lived through it barely.
Jonas prayed while running
away from the burning
call of you.

The prayer of Jacob was
a divine wrestling all night,
a going on with blessing in
his ears, limping in his legs.
Tortured Job's prayer was
of manure, flies, cruel fate
and the theology chatter
of his preacher friends.
Prayer for Moses was the struggle
that ripped him away
from the shepherd peace
he wanted so desperately.
Jeremiah sought only a
middle-class life, a wife,
some ground to call his own.
Prayer for him was cursing
out God from jail.
Habakkuk prayed by asking
why believe in one whose
holy promise history mocks.
Paul had it out with God
over the thorn in his flesh
and all he ever got was "no".
We would learn to pray, O Lord,
yet we shrink from true
coming to terms with you.
Help us to and through
Gethsemane, be with
our wrestling, our grappling
with destiny and you.
You know well what a
horrid place is prayer.
Coax us into this holy line
of battered men who
got through to you
and found themselves.

I bought a new suit a couple of days ago, and I'd like to tell you about the strange thing that happened. I had put the suit on and I stepped into the store's three-walled mirror. I was looking straight-ahead at the cut of the cloth and the way it hung in front and whether the trousers fit. When I turned to look at the side view I was suddenly and for a flash stunned to see not me, but a stranger standing there in a new olive suit. He had a funny-shaped head and he needed a haircut and his shoes had worn-down heels. It was me. But it was a me I hadn't seen before and there was a second of almost terror at being confronted by someone staring away who was me. I wanted to touch him, this stranger, but there was glass and more that held me back. I wanted to speak to him, but there were no words. The feeling lasted for only a fraction of a second and it was gone. Thinking about it since, I have realized that such a moment of fear and of yearning was not unfamiliar to me. I have bumped into the stranger before. In a way this collection of prayers is tribute paid to that

stranger. In some way I am bumping into him now as I write these words for you; perhaps you are bumping into a stranger of your own. We are strangers to each other because we are strangers to ourselves.

The pages of this book are the hangover of one hard question; must we accept our strangeness, our inability to communicate with ourselves, with each other, with God? I am not the first man to ask this question, just as we are not the first men to lash out at the way we find things to be. We are not the first men to nearly strangle in crossed wires. Thousands of years ago there were no wires to be crossed, but there were men like us. One of them, a poet, looked around and saw–as we do, when buying suits and at other times—that men are strangers to themselves, to each other and to God. That poet told a story about the strangers and how they got to be that way.

The poet was the author of the Book of Genesis, and the story he told was the story of the tower of Babel. Men were not always strangers. There was a time when "all men spoke the same language—even with the same vocabulary." But those men rebelled against God and against each other. They tried to build a tower to heaven. They tried to become God. But only God is God and those men lost their unity of language and understanding. They became confused, both within and without. They became strangers to each other, to themselves and to God. And they became—through time—us.

In this story, using language as his symbol, the author of Genesis describes what we suffer from. We have a confused language, you and I. We are born with a constitutional inability to communicate. Our words cannot do the job, for what we yearn to share is ourselves and there are no words. One person, feeling deep and awesome fullness, speaks the word "love" to another—who thinks of toothpaste on television. We find all too often that the words we use are empty, running like rats' feet over broken glass. And perhaps worse even than crossed wires is the feeling that the wires are unplugged. I experience my isolation most when I hear a true word from another person, and all I feel are the inner eyes of my stranger staring, staring out from me to you. And neither of us knows why.

We are born to this confusion, this isolation, this awful living alone in a world of strangers. I am aware of at least two reactions to it. The first one, which I am only lately coming to recognize as my own, is anger. I don't like feeling trapped, but I feel trapped and I don't know why. I feel like I have a right not to be confused. I am angry at the you who reads this because you confuse me and cut me off. I am angry at the You who is God because he has called me to this and it is too hard. The author of Genesis makes the Lord sound so cynical, and I say to myself, "Yes, He must be the great cynic; what a grotesque thing to do!" I feel at times that God is my enemy.

Feeling like this I have to ask why? Why are my yearnings after you so furious? I don't know, unless it is that love so often can't get through. And this is the second reaction we have to our situation—our great need to get through, to overcome our brokenness and isolation. To find unity and, yes, love. This is what drives all men mad, this quest for a new word that will uncross all wires and reconcile us with ourselves, each other and God. All men are driven by this need for unity. All of us are yearning after some you. We run up a hundred blind alleys, dial a million wrong numbers. Some find the charm of union and reconciliation between themselves and men, themselves and God, themselves and their strangers, in chemicals, whether alcohol or drugs. One of the blind alleys I have run up has been to hide behind a mask in a kind of aloof detachment. My blind alley is symbolized by an adventure I had one summer in New

York City. I was literally a clown in a literal parade. I masked my face in greasepaint and wore a costume and ran laughing and singing down 9th Avenue. Thousands of people hung out from their windows and waved at me. I had found the new language. I was laughed at and loved, but when the greasepaint came off the mask didn't. The tragedy of seeking unity and communication in chemicals or masks or any of a million other ways is that, in the end, we find ourselves more alone than ever. Ninth Avenue for me now is the lonliest street in the lonliest city in the world.

All of this brings me to the good news at the heart of these prayers. My own story doesn't end with the falling of my tower of Babel. It has been continued by my falling in love with certain people, some Paulist brothers, some friends at the Georgian Clinic in Atlanta, some at Boston University, some others. It has been continued by some of them, somehow, falling in love with me. And that makes me feel like either I am drunk or the holy spirit of God has seized me and caught me up, and, glory be to God, it is Pentecost again. What happened at Babel, when all men were dispersed and divided into different languages and warring cultures, has been reversed. People came, according to the poet who wrote the Book of Acts, from all over the world: Parthians, Medes, and Elamites and Mesopotamians. And the word they heard was not confusion but was understood by all. The wires were uncrossed. And, like us, those men couldn't believe it was happening. How did they account for the strange sense of union they felt? They said, "Those fellows are drunk!" But Peter stood up and said, "No! We are not drunk (for it is still morning and we don't get drunk till evening). What you see and hear and feel is the spirit of the Lord pouring himself out on you. And who is the Lord? The Lord is Jesus of Nazareth. He is the Word made flesh so that all words will work. He is God's new language, a language of union and understanding and love. He is the language that can be spoken by all men.

What I want to say to you is that I have seen this vision, and I have worked at catching some of it between these covers. Oh, it has only been moments here and there, but I have seen the outpouring of the spirit. Strange moments when my words and the words of another were empty and confused as ever, and yet the word was made flesh and pitched his tent around us. And at those times I knew in a whole new way what it is to be a Christian, to be part of this sharing community in which the spirit blows softly wherever he wills. Another's being free has freed me. And my freedom has freed another. And the good news is—it is me and you, screwed up and confused and alone and as angry as we are. And the good news is that God is not the enemy, but God is love. He is this thing that happens between us.

But there is still and ever bad news. Pentecost doesn't happen every day. The Tower of Babel seems to. After all the awesome things I have said about love and unity and reconciliation I am battered by certain facts. As a people we are brutally at war. As a community of believers, we are torn apart and polarized, most often in the name—strangely—of Jesus Christ. As individual men we find that we still have to hide. Each of us is a cluster of dreads and uncertainties and hates. The stranger in me and in you hates love and fears it because love and the spirit of God annihilates our world and destroys all our complacent plans. I do want to communicate. I want these words that are born of my cluster of ambiguities to be received. But I wonder, will this communication destroy me? To fall from that tower of isolation, to fall in love, is really to fall. And we never know whether this time we might hit bottom. And we know—further and most awfully—that no human love lasts. We know that we must die.

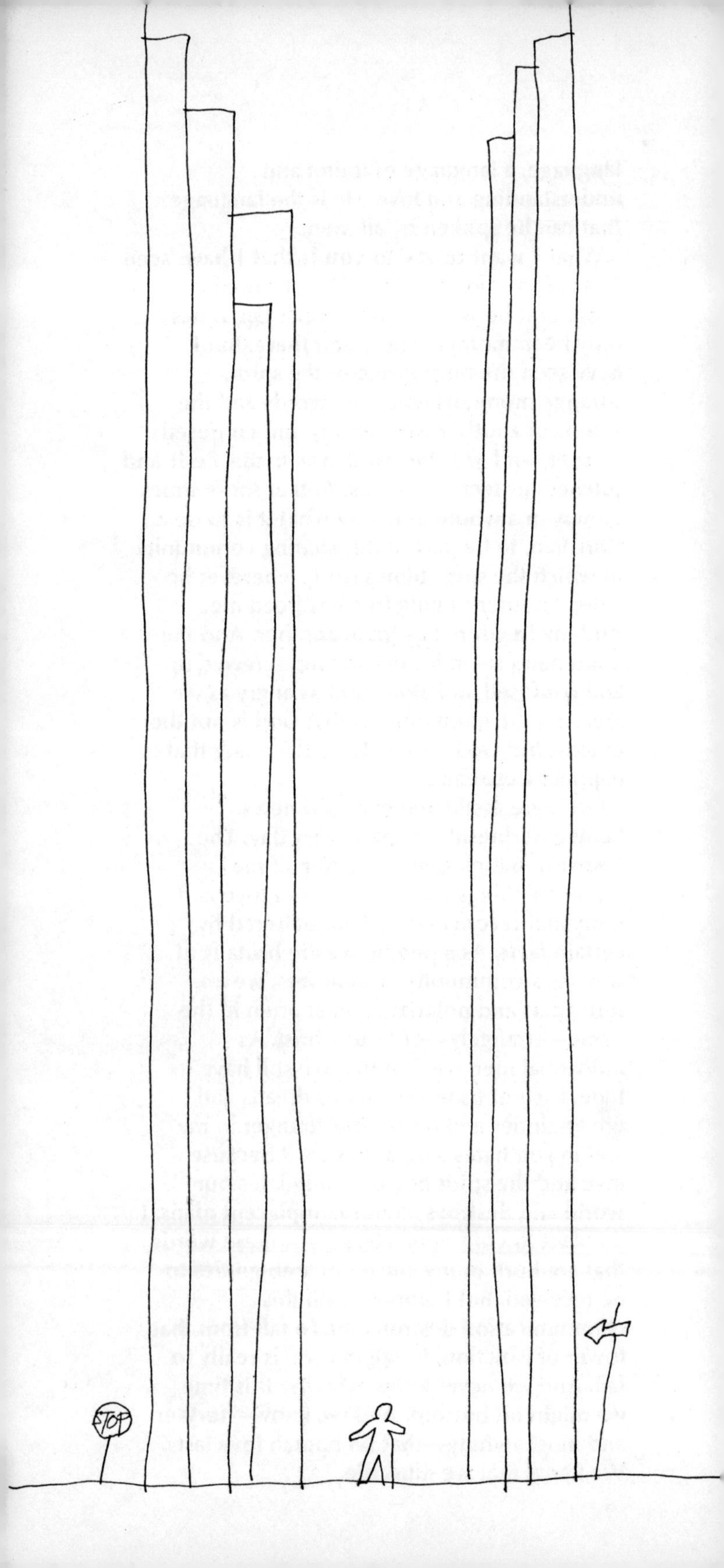
STOP

And so out of all these fears and more, we hold back. We stay put in our willed isolation and wordlessness. When we are in the midst of true communion with someone we run because we are so afraid.

One day, after working over these prayers, I took a walk to clear out the webs. I was walking on railroad tracks that run nearby. I found myself crossing a big gulch on a narrow two-track bridge. When I was about half-way across the bridge I heard a whistle blowing behind me. I knew a train was coming. I froze for a moment at the thought of meeting a train on that high bridge, that high narrow bridge. I felt terror begin to well its way up inside me. I began to run awkwardly because the railroad ties were spaced with air. I was afraid of the coming train. I was afraid of falling through the tracks. I was afraid.

We are afraid like that at times in relationships, when it seems like a solid bridge is built and you're half-way there. But what if we fall? And don't we hear distant whistles all the time? And so we run, all of us, for all we are worth. But, and this is the best news of all, God runs too. And he pours himself out, not just on you and me, but on you and me running. St. Paul wrote that God saves us again and again. He gives us his new language of one true Word made flesh, and he does it again and again. He replaces Babel with the Pentecost spirit of sharing, and he does it again and again. So that each of us, today and tomorrow and every time we bump into a stranger, ours or someone else's, everytime the wires cross, we can think back on whatever Pentecost has been for us and say, "Do it again, God. Do it again and again and again. Amen."

"We are filled with joyful trust in God,
through our Lord Jesus Christ through whom
we have already gained our reconciliation."

Romans 5,11

O God, reconciler, uniter,
bringer together,
I lay my divided self before You.
I have two theologies,
two responses to You
and they capture
the torn-apart of me.
I know that you love
me freely, without price,
for who I am,
not for what I do.
Yet I am frenzied
in my need to earn
your love, to pay for it
with works, achievements.
I know that you make
all things good,
that you swear by
the flesh of your son

that my flesh and self
are good, accepted.
Yet I am ashamed
of who I am, caught
by second thought,
unable to accept
much less love
the very quirks
which make me of me
and loved of you.
I know all men
are received into you
and your firey embrace.
Yet I do not trust
other men, even friends,
with my meagerness,
except at times
seemingly by accident.
I know also that
these inconsistencies
are enouh of me
to be part of you.
Help me to be almost
as little put off, confused
and repelled by them
as You are. And help
me on occasion to find
with surprise that my
two theologies are one.

"If anyone believes in me,
even though he dies, he will live."

John 11,25

If only I could believe it, God,
that you love me as much as You say.
Enough to climb out of yourself
and prowl the cold backstreets of time,
enough to shed the warm garb that is God
and find with a chill that you're naked,
enough to work with hands at fishing and wood
and slowly rebuild the fire within,
enough to burn with flames that slowly grow
and finally jump back into God.
Enough to remember still what you'd become
and so send the Smolder to spread your thaw,
enough to return the furnace of your Father's love
with fire enkindled by one of God,
continued by one of us.

II

If only I could believe it, Jesus,
that even the snow is burning now
in a flame so gentle no flake melts.

I can believe some of the snow,
knowing a million pieces fall
to let three moment on my outstretched tongue
I believe it when the morning says
that barren trees blossom whitely
and that gutters are good afterall.
But You tell me that
You planned from all eternity
to show me with three snowflakes
that I am not alone.
Perhaps at last I'll believe it, God,
when I settle on the warmth
of the tongue that You outstretch.
Catch me.

"You will hear and hear again,
but not understand."

Matthew 13,14

Who's there?
That cry again, quick and unknown
dots the happy sounds I make.
"Help me". Who calls so near?
I shrink my smile and listen,
faint tumblings of a struggle.
Who? I listen and hear
"air, despair", words new to my content.
I squint, lean and cup my ear.
"Help me", savage cry unsheathed.
Someone kicks in my chest, I shudder.
He climbs over my lungs, stumbles
and shouts again, "air",
Who's there?
The sound of panting, his or mine?
I plug my ears and cannot see.
The scream rends, not in, but me.

II

How can I presume to call it He?
the echo-place, its wild hedges
that finger out to prick me from within
several time a year or twice a day?
And how can I presume to call it He,
the other side of sky, which after all
could well be just the empty space
between old bricks of some great house?
And how can I presume when wise men say
that calling doesn't matter, there is no one.
When I myself have said as much
beneath cold sheets when I alone could hear?
Perhaps I've been a fool and now must say
that prickings from within are only that,
must say out loud there is no He but me.
But how, O God just how, can I presume?

PRAYER FOR UNTROUBLED PEOPLE

"I, I am the Lord. Besides me there is no savior."

ISAIAH 43,11

Pity the perfect ones
who never have been lost
in fruitless torments of
"Why for God's sake this?"
Pity the husbands, wives
who never mourn
the loss of a oneness
they never truly had.
Pity the preacher
whose words have never
rung with emptiness.
Pity the unangry man
who never shook at the
release of sudden power.
Pity the teacher
with every answer
and no confusion ever.
Pity the brave
who never cower cold
with fear to sink

a charging fleet of hearts.
Pity the well-dressed
who never quiver naked,
exposed body and self
to another's red gaze.
Pity them all, O Lord.
Coax them out of hiding
into the dread-full circle
of creaturehood, of being man,
of, oh, knowing it so.
You lost yourself in us
O Lord, quivered naked,
troubled, sick save sin.
In your lostness we
are finally found.
When our sanity goes,
as it is doing now,
your sense is ours.
There is you for us.
Pity those who never fail
for they do not taste
the great unfailing you.
They are never battered
in the dear torment
of this desperate love
whether of you or other
failures like your Son.
Pity the perfect, Lord
and when all are
disclosed at the end
let it be that we
did not too pretend.
For now, let us stand
as we surely will then
troubled, stunned, naked,
failing and found by You.

"Love comes from God."

1 John 4,7

The love I lift up is not the panting face
of sentimental joy or misery,
but the easy breathing
of densely human things.
It is the power, often unexpected,
of several people who cope near me
with the business of every day.
There are sudden kindnesses,
unmerited, unhoped for and precious,
when veils of my friends and me
are lifted by an unexpected breeze
of live sharing and soft gift.
This love, made of small words and signs,
is too ordinary to transform time,
to stop the sway of low humdrummings.
But something is unleashed at times
of commonplace love between friends,
a power over us of vision and recall.
A power not overpowering but stirring,
rousing, awakening, respecting us
and making finally, no difference
and therefore all the difference in the world.

II

We see your face, God, in the faces
of our surprising friends.
Love in all our many kinds of family
is the common human word, the only word
we have for the exuberant
and quick-powered life that is you.
In the ones, my friends, who love me
I hear the voice of you
burst strangely in again on everyday.
I am newly reminded, God,
of your abiding, persistent call,
of your exquisite, sighing patience,
of your waiting to be in me
a freeing word of love for other men.
Stir me up again, Oh God,
into your lively kind of ordinariness.
Accept my too reluctant thanks
for what it is; a plea
for yet more common, unexpected love
both to and from your son, your me.

"I, for my part, like things growing in the garden of God, put my trust in God's love for ever and ever."

Psalm 52,8

He loves me said the daisy.
He loves me not it said.
And there I stood
between two piles
of plundered petals.
They were hoarse with
shoutings at each other.
I could hardly hear.
There was a final whisper
from the last
and livest petal.
He loves me it said,
falling dead.
And I was stunned,
looking down at the
naked plucked stem
of myself
and I thought

what a funny way,
torn apart and loved,
to die.

II

You made me once the handsomest
water lily in the pond.
Oh, I was green and gifted
with a certain way of floating.
From farther, even,
than the shore, pollen
and other lightest things
would come to rest
on the cellophane softness of me.
Oh, I was green and gifted!
And it was, I know, You
who made me so.
What, God, of now
and my nothing-head
nakedness thin?
Your plan is well known
for autumn things,
but what of a single
summer water lily
gone early in August
leafless and dry?

"I trembled to the core of my Being,
then I rose to open to my Beloved."
Song of Songs 5,5

A flash of blond on the path ahead,
tossing hair of a book-hugging girl.
We move together in our after-class stride,
two strangers about to meet and pass.
The flash of her hair, the click of her step,
the first faint hint of her smell—
these bridge the last few yards
and prod me alive to a half-second's wonder.
Wonder at the million other moments,
million other meetings bursting out in this one.
Here with me because of some casual word,
because of a father's hidden savings,
because years ago another girl dropped a book
and even longer ago and farther away
an old man died with too many debts.
Now, with me, after unnumbered farewells,
after random wanderings that began
in forests, deserts, mountains, waters.
Random wanderings that have stopped here
and born this afternoon meeting on a path.

We draw close, the path is narrow, I shift.
I feel my face full of smile,
I feel hello running up walls of throat
chased by the leap of my heart
at the years, people, toothaches and tears.
We meet, her eyes drop, her step quickens
and as we pass our coats don't even brush.

II

God of many meetings,
let us break our brokenness on You.
We are born masters of the averted eye.
We can run and step aside at once.
We kill each other with unaltered strides.
But why tell You, are You surprised?
It is not You, God, who is hidden
but everyone of us, hidden by habit.
You alone can find us out, unhide us
as You unhid Your Son Jesus Christ.
We believe it, God, and beg to be found,
to be interfered with, slowed down.
And if we ask this here, listen now
and not later when we try to brush by.

"See I have branded you
on the palms of my hands."

Isaiah 49,16

There is a thing I cannot catch
because it is too near,
but also too near for not grasping at,
though hidden in fear, deep, full, down.
I make pictures or find them made
of heavy-cloaked visitors,
of early flowers daring to unfold,
lingering hours with faint rain,
moonlight laughing in someone's hair.
There are closings and grand openings
but I can never catch the very near,
the very most hidden and dear,
no matter how many, how more are the
seizures of seeing the uncloseures of me.
O God, be not always so near.
I would make no idol, no new cow,
but how can I continue in such nearness
if always it only is the moon splitting itself.
O God, I say it plainly for once; let
Your Self of my self on occasion be caught.

"God has put us at the end of His parade."
1 Corinthians 4,9

Around the always wet corner of my eye
a parade, loud, clear at last, undeniable
keeps promising faintly to come bursting out.
I lean from the window of all my days
but the most that ever makes it
is that Clown, sometimes, of You, O God.
Your fool with an up-down, smile-frown mouth
sent ambiguous to clashing cymbals
that chase the pigeons of my head
from old, stale bread routine.
There are occasional soft moanings
of a tuba, fat and awful, far away,
a whistle, shrilling when it blows
chaos into an order yet to come.
Some brisk drummer reminds at times
unseen marchers of one happy purpose.
I hear it all from my many windows,
desperate, straining my inner ears,
God, to the still inner eye of You.
But the eye of You clashes too
and never turns the corner finally
into the we of us parade.

II

God, we are a parade-chasing people.
Your son, our Clown, danced in pain
through deadly broken fits of ambiguity.
You placed Him at the head of your parade,
a whistle man and drummer for us all.
We believe this, but clashings of many kinds,
symbols or bodies or passions or bombs,
make way-back stragglers often of us.
We lose sight of your Son, of Your parade.
We run to up catch, remembering,
but wind is short and we tire.
Up catch us, God. Breathe your wind for us.
And, until the Parade of the Day arrives
straggle your foolish Son back here with us,
for the chase gets old. We could use a smile.

"My spirit fails me, but you"

Psalm 142,3

I come and I go, I begin
and begin to begin again.
I try a book of several starts,
then, again, a promised piece of writing.
I try checking the sky for rain
then checking the rain for sky.
I think of a loved of mine,
then think of maybe a little beer.
Which is good but makes me hungry.
I try the book, then to write.
I see some dirt to wipe,
a shirt to hang, a door to shut.
I go outside. I come in. I sit.
I walk, I look at ceiling paint.
There are several peelings to watch.
I begin again to begin at last,
with a screwed-up will to finish.
Then I remember with some urgency
the morning's uncapped toothpaste.

II

God, when boredom smothers me,
when my spirit sucks in and blows away,
You are, I fear, no more or less
than any other tug of insignificance.
You are an unbegun book to me,
or, if begun, abandoned ten times and more.
You, like an old icebox, are come to
and gone from slightly chilled.
You are tasted and put down,
tested and many time turned from.
God, be a coaxer out of me
of some interest, slight vigor,
a bit of consistent enthusiasm.
While doing so, if You will,
be patient with my faithless,
fickle and childish frenzy.
I can't say I enjoy it either,
and would, with help, yes, change.

*"The Word was made flesh
and we saw his glory."*

John 1,14

**I was a running stream
of church-words, god-talk,
a litany of language
about salvation, hope,
grace, redemption, faith,
forgiveness, love, law,
dogma, trinity, omnipotence,
glory, promise, prayer . . .
So many words,
much exhaled air.
Then one day I met
this fairly grey fellow
who happened to live
in my piece of world;
quite an ordinary man,
veteran, college grad,
Cincinnati-born,
prone to easy blushing,
awkward at first meetings,
movie goer, book reader,**

not much for baseball . . .
Ordinary, but somehow
now, in looking back,
different to this extent;
certain words were flesh
in him for me,
and what I know is that
grace and love
and salvation and acceptance
are more than exhalings
now, and he served
as my blind fingers
for those raised words
and I beheld some glory.

II

Lord, when your Word is made flesh
in those who share our world,
in the ordinary men we know
and drink coffee with and love,
then, then, Lord, do all the words
leap from their sleep.
Your acceptance of us as we are
becomes touchable through theirs,
and we, blind, need it so.
Then, Lord, only then do we behold
your glory, when your Word
makes Himself flesh again
in the common pale flesh of men.

"I have told you this so that my own joy
may be in you and your joy be complete."
John 15,11

Who, if not you, O Lord, could grant
such piercing happiness as this?
Mine is the joy of pure "a-ha",
of surely some revelation at hand,
of a nearly second coming.
Mine is the joy of the daybreak sentry
or of a little boy whose new toy
is a real flashlight and all kinds
of bugs and flying pieces of dust
and tiny spider webs that never
were there before this birthday.
I have been dipped again in you, O God,
and have been shown again
the course of mine and other times.
Mine is the joy of the man
who brings to the table
tomatoes he has grown himself
and in a single moment savors
not only the reddest food
but all the hard days

and every crisp morning
since the soft and secret planting
a whippoorwill ago, an age;
the amber evening waterings,
the callous cuttings back
and all the inch by inch
pleasure of seeing it grow.
This is clearly a moment
of some other making than mine.
You, O God, it is You, O God
who have graced me, gifted me,
made me mute again
with a spark of your vastness
that is, as You say, unwinding
itself in my days of growing
and threading itself into
a future of absolute You, me
all my others and song.

"Now these are your people
whom you have redeemed."

Nehemiah 1,10

Take any crowd,
look closely at it.
See the wire fine
of fear that joins
us jumbled people.
A student has just
failed the last
and crucial test.
A wife worries sick
over her young marriage.
A distinguished grey
man of some means
trembles under new
sexual fantasies of night.
A thirtyish single
blond wonders whether
some man will yet.
A preacher can't believe
his own old words.
A salesman, slowing down,

needs another early
drink for many roads.
A nursing home widow
forces angry loneliness
into powdered sweetness.
There is a baker whose
life is day-old bread.
An old rag bum
has bagged his bones
and is coming guilty
off another drunk.
A colored maid
splurges her child's
dinner on busfare, late.

These are jumbled
people pieced together
into each one of us,
for each of us
carries a heavy crowd,
knowing it or not,
in the dark of his eyes.
These, no others, are
the very ones for whom
joy himself has died
the strange fearful death
of this jumbled daily life.

"Even after this I seemed to hear the great sound of a huge crowd singing 'Alleluias' "

Revelations 19,1

When May, strange month,
is grieving under
leaves heavy, bowed by
many Mondays mourning
and headaches of
low clouds everywhere
about to spill down
silent child tears;
when cheeks in many
small rooms wait
alone and baffled for
the slow, greasy flood
of creeks run together
in the world's last wetting;
when death looks out
from the deepest place
in the bluest eyes, and
when, strangest thing,
the eyes are mine
and well they see

why am I young still
and very, very glad?

II

God, there are times when gladness
makes no sense yet is there
pure and unaccountable and wild.
How can I be glad, yet believe
as I do in death and maybe death,
if not because I believe as well
in life and maybe, God, in You?
I take unnecessary joy as a token,
a gift, a sign from You,
and infiltraton of hope.
I accept it as the task
You tell me—by giving—it is.
I will be unnecessary joy,
the strange thing, for some other
griever like me under May,
and I, with a boost from You,
will click my heels at death.

"Then the Lord said, 'I am going to measure my people by plumb-line' "

Amos 7,8

**Measure if you must, Lord,
but we can tell you now that
you will find a strange mixture
of common men. A few
among us are good men.
Some are evil, who bear your name.
But most are never either
like most men most places.
We are builders, trowels in hand
but guns loaded, loosely holstered.
Some of us are here for love
of you and every brother,
but most out of restless curiosity,
for want of a better temple.
We are men of moderation
in both virtue and vice,
which is to say we
maintain a pale neutrality.
We have an allergy to risk.
We don't often fail,**

but then we don't often
try, which is only common sense.
We are a safety-first people.
We are finger-nail clippers.
We are drab strangers.
O God, Help us.

II

If truly we are your people
Color us incarnation!
Out of slimy mud of first chaos
you brought meaning and creation.
Out of confused Babel folk
you brought a pentecost speaking,
loud shouting people of joy.
Out of us surely you can
do it all again, drab or no.
Take our commonness, our
curiosity, our restlessness,
our indecision, our neutrality,
our musty moderation;
Do your windy hovering
and quicken us again.
Give us safety last, riskability.
Make us wild with You
enough at times to be taken
for mid-morning drunks. Amen.

"Yahweh says this; if you could break
my covenant with the day and my covenant
with the night so that day and night
do not come at their due time
then my covenant with my servant
might also be broken."

Jeremiah 33,20

O God, I surprise myself
continuously, monotonously!
I make nightness of nearly
every day, noon high or not.
I catch the amazing light
of pure offered love and
dye it in the shadow
vat of willed isolation.
As nightmakers go
I must rank with the
twilight giant, the snuffer-out
the stuffer-down of sun
into the bag for get-away.
But having gotten gone, where?
On what scaffold do we,
the snuffers-out of sun,

stand and, finally, lie?
O God, take this one old
night creature making,
do him the morning trick,
coax him into childhood
of the light, uneternal infancy
of eternal early day.

"Lord, hear my prayer . . . my spirit fails me
and my heart is full of fear.
Quick, Lord, answer me."

Psalm 143,4

Fear is numb clawing
within my lungs,
the low moaning
from back of hidden
unopened doors that seem
at times not to be mine,
but are, I know.
I am afraid, not only
of death, the common fear,
but of, even, daily darkness.
My inner crumbling
climbs some cliff and stares
with second eyes at blackness.
The future is the longest
night of all, darkest,
most unknown, naked.
Will I be able,
will I have strength,
will I be unbroken

by whatever sudden monster
waits in the dark
of all my tomorrows
for this throat of mine?
When, as now, my heart
is heartless, my spirit
out of breath as fear
threads its uncertain way
through my courage,
what can be soil for me
of some certitude?
Quick, quick answer!

II

"A new heart I will give you, and a new spirit
I will put within you . . .
I will put my own spirit within you." Ez. 36, 26

I may be mistaken
but I believe I hear
the shiver of daybreak.
"I am", it says, "a new
heart for you. I am
desperate arms around you.
I cannot say 'have no fear',
only, 'have no fear alone';
let there be in
your shuddering before dark
and all uncertainties
something of hope,
something of daybreak,
something of, yes, me."

"I mingle my drink with tears."

Psalm 101,10

**I happens, not often,
but happens that my eyes
sink slightly in heaviness
that is both wet and bashful.
My eyes sank today,
I was not surprised
for I have been strangely
heavy for some time.
But my eyes kept sinking
and I was surprised
when a twilight ocean
wrecked itself on me.
I had never wept before,
had wished, but never.
Thunders of all my days
shook out of me,
waves of hope broke
themselves violently on
silent deep-down fear,
silent deep-down fear.
I had never wept before.**

I had never wept before.
Today my eyes sank,
my breath lost itself,
my shoulders rolled away
on the sunken-eyed tide
of the everlasting sea
of soft waters of joy
that my straining sorrow
borrowed then for tears.

II
O Lord, let this be written for me and all;
you looked down from your holy height
and you saw all the earth and me;
and you saw me weeping
and you saw that it was good.
O God, I find it near impossible
truly to weep for I am made ashamed
by magazines of my weakness,
of the helpless, lonesome child in me.
I have cried to you in stifled ways before,
have asked to be opened and freed.
You have heard my begging, Lord,
you have released me from my self,
set free this child of weakness and fear,
and You have not despised it
as I have so long done.
You have let me cry,
have let me shudder openly
the hidden shudder of my heart.
I praise you for my breaking down
and for your breaking down
my brokenness in tears.
You have accepted me, O God,
in weakness and in strength.
Knowing that perhaps now I too
can accept this child in me,
this child in faith of you.

"I, Yahweh, let my tenderness yearn"
Jeremiah 31,30

**Be tender of wishes,
cling like leaves to
chain-link fences
in winter wind.
Wishes have whipped
small hurricanes
of memories that
blow from inside
link-wrinkled eyes.
Wishes are window
panes of cellophane;
breathe softly on them,
make messages with
touchings of your nose.
If of nothing else,
be tender of wishes, a tender be,
for God-made-man,
the wish that worked,
clings like leaf's breath
wishing to work again.**

II

God, we make wishes of our own
for, first of all, tenderness ever
from You and, occassionally at least,
for tenderness from us for us.
We wish for soft breathings of peace
and strong winds of understanding.
We wish for touchings of reconciliation,
for good memories to keep in wrinkled days.
We wish for Your Wish Himself,
for his tender and tangible presence soon.
Until then may we His tenders be
since You, O God, are tender so to us.

"Then the angel took the censer
and filled it with fire and
threw it down to earth . . .
and the earth shook."

Revelations 8,4

If you are God
you kindled me;
my wooden world,
this darkened stable
bright-fired with
faith's funny fable
burns to the clamor
of caught infinity.
I wait for smoke
to clear to see
how your-sent flames
can lap at wood
and tear and kill
and still be good.
I wait, soot-black,
trying not to flee.
If you are God
then fire builds beneath

this crumbled pile
of stable ash.
If not no spit,
no curse is rash.
We are dead and wear
time's only wreath,
the sounds of charred
and gnashing teeth.

"While we were yet sinners
Christ died for us."

Romans 5,8

A deformed and ugly child
lives deep in the sea of each of us,
always newly born and ours.
We are fathers, mothers of sin,
of eternal, twisted secrets
from which, eyes covered,
we flee down passages of fear.
It is in each of us
what we ourselves cannot forgive,
what we cannot claim as us.
For me the child of ugliness
is my constitutional inability
to love without motive.
I would be still running,
still writhing with quiet horror,
still hiding in the garden
of my fallen fatherhood
behind foliage of green distraction.
I would be fleeing my child
but for good news I have.

The deformed and ugly
new-born of me has been
taken up, coddled, embraced,
lullabied and kissed.
God himself took arms
and lips and learned to sing
to love me for myself.
All of who I am, my ugly
and the runner away in me
have been accepted, forgiven, loved.
While I was yet deformed
from a cross Christ kissed my
and every man's ugliness
with slow, breaking tenderness.
Now such is this news
we can dare take into our arms
ourselves; we can bow over
all ugliness and coddle it.
You can kiss the secret in me
and I, gently, in you.
We can, with the Lord's
man-kissing father, O God!,
coddle and kiss ourselves.

"The Lord says, 'I take no pleasure
in your solemnity."

Amos 5,21

When my heart is shuddering
and I no longer know
how to contain this passion
of death for life,
the sight of someone,
a young mother say,
who is content within
the narrows of simplicity,
who knows how from day to day
to get by and be joy
for her children of laughter,
who, when she sees the fall
of leaves thinks only
that winter is coming,
coal will be needed,
the sight stills the tumult,
calls me back to havens
of peace, acceptance and
hope even for my grim

unlaughing, foolish self.
O Lord if you are half
as grim unlaughing toward
me as I am, neither of us,
if I may dare to say,
has half a snowball's chance.

"My only friend is darkness."

Psalm 87

End of the chapter, drop the book,
slide under the sheets, draw up the spread.
Poised on an elbow, pound the pillow,
stretch for the button that turns
the darkness on and the silence.
The pillow is briefly hollow like some ocean.
The whole room breathes in the blackness.
Stillness at last, no earnest echoes,
words or creaking smiles, none
of the shouted love, whispered hate.
The dark's only sound is the clapping
of its one free hand as day
wrecks itself on night in me.
Warm, yet I shudder and slide further down.
Tired, yet I clench the pillow closer,
Dark, yet I squeeze my eyes out of light.
I push my feet away, stretch at the knees
and will my bodied mind asleep.
All in vain, for the moment is come
and I know again that I am alone.

II

God, I dare to say it -
there is no lonliness like the nearness of You.
There is no darkness like the brilliance of You.
Your light here is a semi-darkness
and I stumble in its shadows.
If it were a noon-day's crystal once
would I see you and my many lovers
or would I be single still, stunned and blind?
Would it, even so, I dare to ask, be worse?
Accept this dark moan of moments alone
as my yearning for You, for true others.
Then make it so, for my moan comes close as now
to being the dark death of love,
of You, of every friend in me.

"God has loved you because
you are a man of desires"

Daniel 10,11

A little boy's first brush with mystery
comes when he decides to be blond
and not red-freckled anymore.
It is then that what is given trails off
and gift confuses itself with circumstance.
I have decided to be immortal,
never to miss slight hints of love,
and always to be gentle with your eye.
I will never let it fade, this flush of care,
I have chosen of desire not to die.
But I, no boy, am still no blond.
And nothing is immortal but mortality.
If married, I would be bald and busy.
Am I left to choose only the shells
of what is already chosen for me?
I have come to this windowpane of asking,
pressed my face against it cool,
watched the rain trace its crooked way
dodging blurred faces, of which one
is wrapped in dim and freckled hope.

II

God of my desires I hope in you.
You are the possible of my impossibility,
the hangnail of all my wishes,
forgotten at times but always there
and somehow always slightly known.
My wishes are wild and often unwillable:
They play havoc with my comfort
and feed me frequent spoons of fear
so regular are their whimsied no's.
I wish for you, God, though I shouldn't
since, as I believe, you are my now.
But, to be sure, I still wish for you
so frightened as well as freckled is my hope.

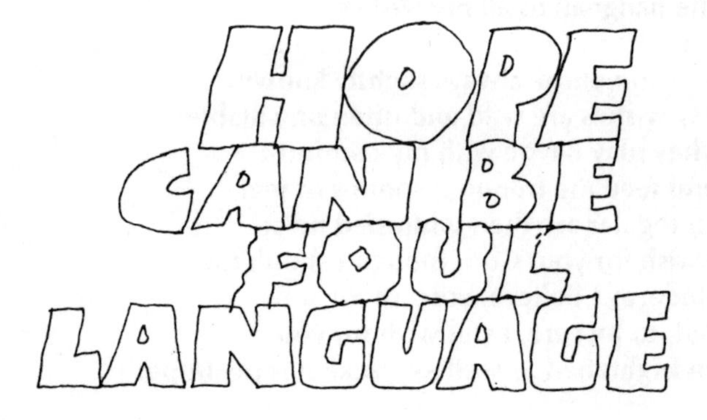

"Come now, let us talk this over," says the Lord. "Though your sins are like scarlet they shall be white."

Isaiah 1,18

This is about a moment
of my making and being
unbowed after breaking
against death alive in me.
Hope was just a word,
always a virtue with
which to cope.
Then hope took flesh
in a man for me,
in whose arms after
certain death I wept.
A short, fattish, tobacco
chewing former farmer,
once a second baseman
in the minors for Detroit.
He walked with me
through the shaded valley
of all my loss, loneliness.
We came through together

and found ourselves talking;
"Chuck", I said,
"I have this passion
to be well-liked."
His cheek was full
and every now and then
he floored a can with spit.
I had begun to think
he had not heard
when he drawled at me
from another world;
"Jesus was so well
liked they nailed
his ass to a pole."

II

Father I give you thanks
for your sons Jesus
and Chuck
who conspire for me
to flesh out hope
and life and other
words of you.
They conspire to hammer
out on me
something of truth
and my own love for me.
Knowing that they and
others give two damns
and more for me
Perhaps I can,
accepting what You
have been saying all
along in a million ways.
God of us all
help me to be who
in You I am.
Help me to be so
for your sake, Chuck's,
several others' and mine.

"This is your fate.
How it pierces your heart"

Jeremiah 4,18

Sometimes, when my feet are wet still
from the dew and willows shiver
in spite of a higher, working sun,
my solitary game perishes, goes awry.
Saturday golf can be too early,
too soon and too, o yes, alone.
At certain such times silence recedes
shore-like behind the small, erratic assault
of club on ball down long
thin bending channels of green.
I find myself thinking to slapping
leather rhythms of heavy walking
that par is too far;
horizons away some can waits
in the soil of gentle, special care.
There is a pang, inarticulate, momentary,
that disipates then the holy rush of coursing.
The sacrifice of sleep, the getting up at dawn
seems flashingly and all at once futile.
Tee to green is one thing, but here to horizons—
there are, as I say, such moments
at times, Saturdays, early, golfing.

II

God, you give me boundary moments
such as this, when I, held-breath,
can see again that I am not You,
that horizons are too far, that I die.
You let me see, God, you let me say
whatever word I choose to make it mean.
I choose You for my only word,
though others are real, perhaps true, at times.
I choose You, God, and give your name
to this magnificent yearning of being man.
I choose You because, from beginning
through years of tears to Saturdays
You have (so you say, so I hear) chosen me.

"It is not good
that the man should be a lone . . ."

Genesis 2,18

From out of the west
in a cloud of dust
came the single most
myth of my once life.
What was important to me
was the silver of the bullets,
the whiteness of the hat
and the hi-ho of the horse.
I bore the name of
a man of strange ways,
hidden origins, a raiser
up of dust and lowly people.
(Picture Tonto in his teepee
nodding to the overture
of a certain William Tell.)
I was caught in kimosabi,
believing, as the Indian
with grunting used to say,

"Better to have face in mask
than to have face in flask."
I thought of myself
as lover well of justice,
bringer-in of outlaws.
My weekly reward
was a mystery martyrdom,
leaving the girl behind,
knowing the townfolk
would wonder who I was.
At the end of each episode
I got this strange delight
chasing far-setting suns,
the mask slightly wet
at my range of being lone.

II

Forgive me my myths, Father,
all of my measely martyrdoms.
It is too easy to claim
the name of servant
when I am slyly served,
to make of my celibacy
a cowboy kind of romance
that feeds both on my need
to be a savior of sorts
and on my fear of love.
For I do fear it, Lord.
If left to myself
I would be left a lone
and well-masked ranger,
riding away just as sun
began to set on my isolation,
and just as two secrets,
mine and one other's,
were about to splash together.
But you, O Lord, have not
left me ever to myself.
You have un-loned me,
melted down by bullets
into silver sons of men
with whom I can stop,
pitch a tent and dwell.

You have done this great
thing of love in me, O God.
Do it again and again
for such is my celibacy,
my priesthood for you,
that there sounds ever the faint
lovely whisper of William Tell.

"I had to be let down over the wall
in a hamper through a window
in order to escape."

2 Corinthians 11,33

Most of my life I lingered in this lofty room,
never left, though I believed with other fools
this loft was just a home of sorts and not a soul.
Only when I lost the key did I find the door
ever locked, thick, unyielding, closed on love.
The only leaning brow on brow, mouth on mouth
of that room from my earliest golden days
had been with a twin in the pool of my dreams.
When I found the key lost, I was dying sure alone,
dying on the wrong page of hope's thin book.
Whatever drives water through hills drove my blood.
Whatever calls colored-petal sighs from April soil
called lucient and live yearning from my soul.
Under some warm glance my dead twin selves
quickened, stirred, cracked into one man at last.
I was a single blade of grass lifting its sharp head
to the blows of rain and I passed for pain.
I know that a man in the listening becomes with help
and much patience from his helper, his own key,
and that the loftiest, lonliest rooms have windows
for being let out. I was hampered and lowered to life.

II

God. I was entrapped in apathy high and aloof.
I wished for nothing, was man of no desires.
I was ever brooding with what barely passed for life.
Presences of several kinds jolted me out of myself
and I have tasted the fresh astonishment
that being alive and a creature of yours at last is.
I give certain names to helpers I had and have,
names of men who call themselves your serving sons,
which is part of why to all this being let down alive
I now give the name of You and say while I can
my thanks. Be a constant hamper to me, God,
and be so always with such loving lowerers
as I, your new lively son, have these days known.

"One day he said,
'What shall I compare
the kingdom with?' "

Luke 13,18

Being me
is sometimes
as if a contest
had been held once
is a somewhere
sort of place
with the promise of
a million magic
prizes of infinite
glitterings of
joy's reward,
as if the contest
had been held
and God above
God of love
I won.

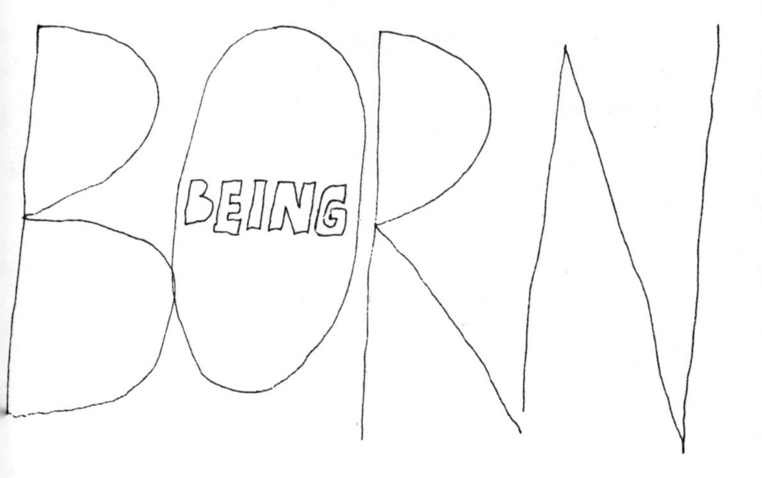

"From the beginning till now
the entire creation has been groaning in
one great act of giving birth,
and not only creation, but all of us"

Romans 8,23

Quicker my kickings, quicker,
louder the throbbings around me;
I am about to be born,
to leave this sea of water and blood
that has kept me warm and alive
yet bound as by a cord.
Oh, for breathing and running
and knowing at last who carries me,
knowing with more than my blind bumpings
or the occassional probings by someone
outside the walls of my world.
I love the one whose blood I drink,
whose fingers press to see
if yet there beats a heart in me.
But in my pounding suffocation
I breathe only my bearers breath
and I would see the face.

II

God, I would uncramp these arms
of mine and fast would find
the neck of You I know is waiting.
Oh, for the joy these pangs promise,
the smokeless air, the knowing You
and all for whom I am so blind,
to whom I am so bloody bound.
God, coax me out of groaning
my womb-like indifference,
out of my tomb-like detachment.
I would see Yours and every face,
would have my own be seen.
Oh, let my life be quickened and quick,
and be with me now
and at the hour of my birth, amen.

"We are fools for the sake of Christ."
1 Corinthians 4,10

**Being baptized for real
can be what it is to
discover you've spent the
day with the price tag
still on the seat
of your new trousers.
Everyone knows trousers
have to be new sometime,
but we pretend otherwise.
Being baptized is letting
things appear to be what
they in fact are.
Which may mean admitting
the newness of clothes,
the oldness of certain
practised masquerades
(I favor one young
movie star, myself).
If we can admit
the foolishness that is
no one else's but ours
some of the foolishness
that is God's hidden-wise
may yet sprinkle itself
foolishly on us.**

"For all these mysteries I thank you,
for the wonder of my self,
for the wonder of your works."

Psalm 139,14

Chiefly for
what has been stolen
from death;
a meeting, yesterday,
over coffee
of two ragged men,
me and a fellow
I never liked before.
Thanks to both of you,
God and friend Dave,
for snaring love
out of me.
There was a time
when I would have taken
the very common drippings
of that moment,
the quaver in his voice,
the passing of cream,
the squirming of my eyes,

those clumsy words of evening,
the timid of us both—
would have taken them,
common all, as only common.
But such was the mystery
and such is the wonder
that, over coffee,
was coaxed out
of me and friend Dave
the very most unsought,
uncommon, yet unstrange
kind of beckoning near.
O God, simple new friendship
stole itself out of death
on small, awkward coffee feet
into the crab-grass yard
of my fenced off soul.
There was, out of commonness,
a cathedral built of tissue,
human, mine, Dave's and alive,
a fragile, webbed-together
sacred place of You.

"These sufferings . . . bring hope and
this hope is not deceptive because love,
the love of God, has been poured into
our hearts by the Holy Spirit
which has been given us."

Romans 5,6

What I found, O God,
when I climbed into the skin
of another man
was a view of you
from a high criss-crossed agony.
I remember how it was
when I was all mirrors,
no windows; I resented
people thinking me selfish
when I was only being myself.
But being myself was
so boring and so alone.
What I discovered, O God,
looking out on the world
through borrowed wet eyes
was plain as his pain;
I can love this man,

**can stir up love in him.
I can be your offer of grace,
You can see my hidden face
of joy after years of winter,
now that finally I have stepped
out of your determined way
and let you throw me bodily
into the lonely desparate way
of another lonely desperate man.
I know, God, that this love
pouring awkwardly out from me
was poured gently into me
by you in your Spirit of oneness
through Jesus Christ our Lord.
In and with and through Him
I give you thanks, O God.
When, as even now, I shrink
in fear of loving another man
because I love so poorly if at all,
remember me who does it, Lord,
that it is always you
who does the seizing in joy,
the lifting up together of love.**

"Listen, my son,
to your father's teaching . . ."

Proverbs 1,8

There are strangers living in this house,
quiet with each other, polite and far away.
What is there to say, what words to touch
the deep, soft and common flesh of fear?
Fathers are desperate in their silence to say
that they too worry at coming chaos.
have rebelled at bland and easy answers
that they too worry at coming chaos
Sons are frenzied in their distance to say
that they too worry at coming chaos
and would also save past greatness.
But, in their mutual wordlessness,
father and son hurl mountains of sound,
angry and unhearing, at each other.
Fathers speak only of irresponsibility,
sons only of all the ways the old
stifles the young and twists it.
Soon the sounds have ceased again
and the polarized isolation is done.
The son may vow never to shave

though his young beard will hesitate at first.
The father vows never to discuss again
and goes away without leaving at all.
They separate, joined only by their anger
and a mutual mad of righteousness.
They are fierce in their refusals always,
but for those moments alone at night
when an under-edge of sadness-memory
cuts out a child, gruff-tender hands, and tears.

II

God, father of all sons, uncurse us.
Where we most want unity there is war.
How can a world be at peace if no home is?
We, young and old the same, are frightened
by the deepening now of disunity
between all our fathers, all our sons.
Does love grow feeble; Is trust outgrown?
You, whom we dare call Father, God,
have given to men a man, your son.
We saw him grow and die clinging to you
as if you alone, his father, cared
and could help and we know it was so.
Be Father to us now, to all of us
and make of our fatherhood, our sonship,
the magnificent sharing that is yours
and his always, even now, even ever.
We believe that your sharing is present
and bringing us together now, even now,
that your sharing Breathes among us
as a Spirit of unity, trust and love.
We believe it is so but are torn still
into fearful pieces of cold relatedness.
Let fathers be fathers again or for once;
let sons be truly sons, not strangers.
We ask it with You and Yours before us.

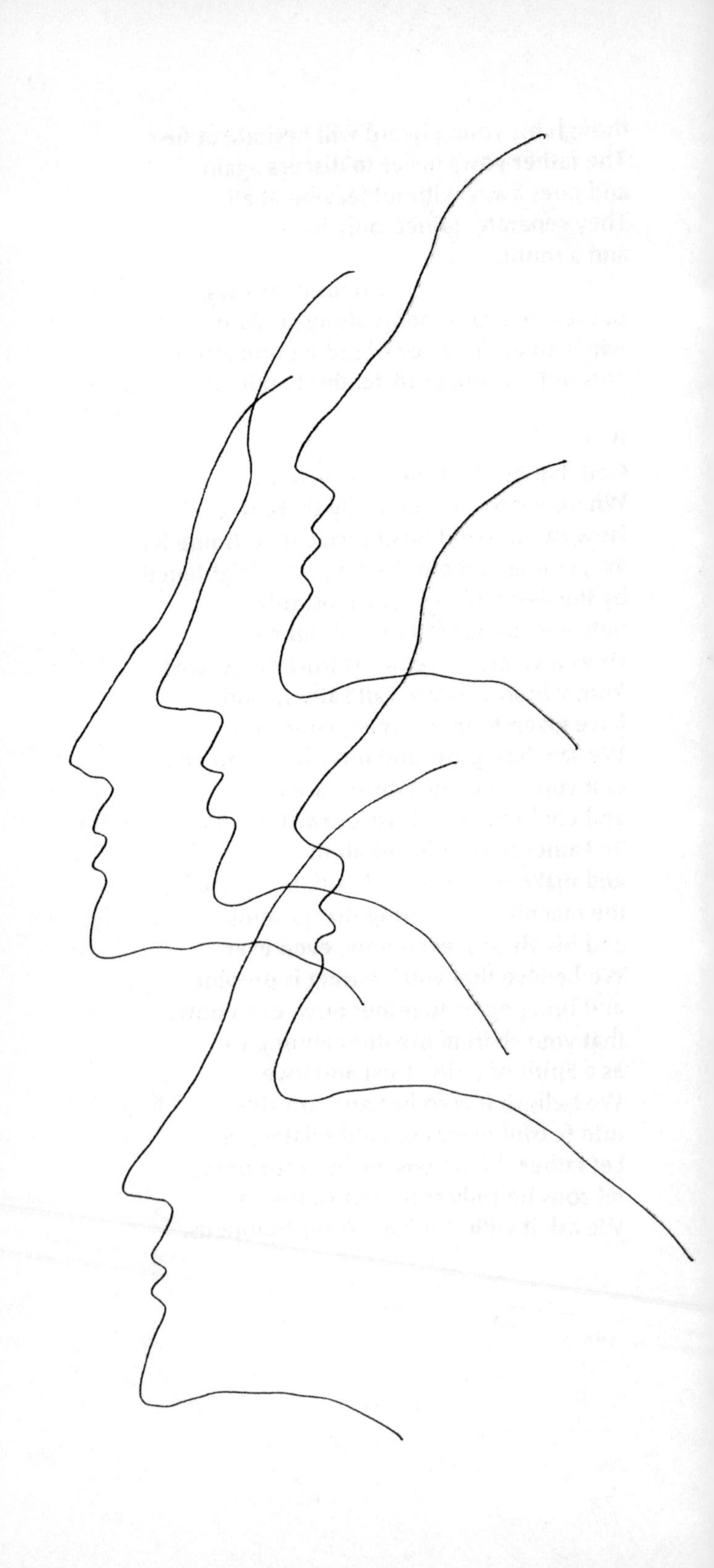

"They were filled and began
to speak in other tongues."

Acts 2,5

We lean, tentative, anxious, together.
We summon courage and small trust,
and with dried voices dare to speak,
to unpierce ourselves, unhide the secret
with carefully chosen and just possible words.
We whisper together, we utter,
but the words are easier than we are
and they run loud and meaningless,
wind through dry grass, shamples of hope,
shod-iron feet through splintered glass.
Words even great and pregnant ones,
have grown up or shrunk or frozen
into yet another obstacle to union of sorts.
Words are yet another sentence, condemnation,
telling us dry and again how alone we are.
It is nearly time for silence always.
We are cheap words longing to be still.
We are, alternately, silence dreaming
of being any spoken word however trite.
What we need, in a word, is a word
that goes both ways and can bear much use.

II

God, there is, we believe, one word
which never was trite or cheapened,
which survives the eternal attempt
to lock it into our predictable vocabulary.
That word is Your son, we believe,
spoken by You from all ever until now,
near us in the flesh of Jesus Christ.
Forgive us our making a lie of him
on our bloody, blaspheming lips.
Speak him again and with both edges
cutting quick through our thick
and cloudy and wordy confusion.
Open our ears to hear him again,
the one pure sound, the one true word,
the one utterance in whom we, men, meet.
Quicken our tongues to speak him yet,
our one hope here for saying something
true and wise, with love and some sense.

"All his friends stood at a distance
and they saw all this."

In parched dry soil
a rose has bloomed.
I never saw it
but so they say.
I've seen soil split
ant-earthquake wise,
jags of nothing
creeking through mud
so hard it hides
whatever rain might
wet have been before.
Roses are red
but everything's dead.
What now?
Where is the seed,
and, worse, where
is the rain?
My soil is parched
my cracks are dry.
God, Father, rain me
something bloomable,
rise me something
roseable.

"He was lifted up while they looked on
and a cloud took him from their sight."

Acts 1,9

They gathered round the man who'd made them friends,
on a hill so high they looked down on small birds
and saw them, shadows, swoop the lake below,
the divings down without the ripples' rings.
They gathered round and felt the usual peace
that lullabied their jealousies to sleep.
His eyes were there through all of them at once,
and all at once could see in them a new
and autumn heaviness that made them think
of old friend summer trees about to leave.
How could it be? He'd gone away before,
those afwul nights of tomb when they had died
and then the day of life's explosion joy,
when rocks rolled back and every eye blossomed.
He'd gone and come again, but what of now?
The very hill was stretched above all sounds.
All wondered in waiting unwanted words,
and then the oldest one suggested bread
but no one moved and he sat down again.

Some moments passed before the master spoke,
and then the words were said and he was gone.
They understood only that they were sad
and that, from hills, the birds below look small.

II

God, we believe in your son, Jesus Christ,
that he came sent by you, a man,
that he did the awesome deed of raising us
by being himself raised-up by Pilate, then by You.
We believe that on some last day he will return.
But God, what, for now, we know best
is simply that he is gone, has left.
We know it because birds are small from hills,
because there is a hole in each of our hearts.
It cries to be filled and calls for his coming.
We believe, as he said, that we are not alone,
that, in fact, the hole of our hearts
is the living, unwounded wind of his Spirit
crying out for You and, now, for us.
Hear, be near and deepen our windy place within.

"The Lord has been like an enemy.
He has destroyed."

Lamentations 2,5

Softly and more certain for her softness
the girl spoke; "That's not my mother."
The father only curled the tip of his tie
and looked down as if to watch it.
Anything but speak or look across the carpet,
as if for fear his wife's crooked foot would show.
A black cigar half-way up his shirt;
it plummeted down like a wedding day rug
and snapped out loud, a tie again.
He has tried to hide from death,
but, unlike his daughter, he knows it.
He has tried to hide from the curse
that is building in his body against God,
against all and every and any that allows
the going into nothing of his dear Martha.
The Lord has been like an enemy to him.
The Lord destroyed this mother, this wife,
the lives of a man and one young girl.
He is blind, inarticulate, sure only of the hole
this death is digging deeper even now.

There are no angels. There is no winged soul.
There will never be a choir again, or joy.
There is only the dry flesh of that body,
a slight smell and tons and tons of nothingness.
He begins toying with his tie again,
as if not to clench and swing his fist.
The Lord has been like an enemy to him.
The Lord destroyed all the easy assumptions
and every certainty but this one;
the wife of his life is nothing now.
Where there was comfortable faith before
there is now nothing but this budding curse
and a hard choice that is being made.
Toying with his tie, the man at last uncurses
himself; the words are low, slow and the same:
"Lord . . . lord . . . lord . . . lord . . . lord . . ."

"They exchanged their glory for an idol.
They forgot God."

Psalm 105,26

His would be the best of happy lives
if only his migrane headaches would stop.
Hers would be bliss and more
if only the children would behave.
Another's would be well-fulfilled
if only his raise came through,
if only the training time was done,
if only the mortgage was paid off,
if only a man would call tonight . . .
We are an everlasting "if only"
and we just know for certain
that the getting at last of health,
more money, a college degree,
a job of some significance,
a different wife, a sober husband,
a teenage sons who listens, . . .
the getting of the next need
will bring us happiness at last,
the happiness that is always
just one small problem away.

We seem not to notice somehow
that small problems have ways
of reproducing themselves in turn
and that for all our earnest
"if onlys" there is never a now
of happiness but only of
reaching over obstacles
for that elusive fantasy
of "if only" after.

II

We find ourselves condemned, God,
on a quite unmythical mountain
to pushing one mammoth boulder
up the merciless slope of time.
We tell ourselves again and again
that the mountain levels off ahead
and we are forever about to rest.
We know, Lord, that there is no
level place, plateau or ledge.
There is only this huge rock,
this mountain, our fellow and You.
But we deny all of what is real
by putting our faith and hope and love
in alternate fantasies of "if only".
We refuse to see slopes for slopes,
rocks for rocks, You for You.
We worship at small plastic altars
of health and money and prestige
and we are not chastened even
by the fact of their failures
to satisfy this yearning we have.
We turn again to You, O God,
knowing that satisfaction is true
only when it is of You and therefore,
for now, when it is not fully seen.
We accept this mountainous journey
and resolve to move along it
without the misplaced trust of "if only",
the making of idols into everything
when alone You are ultimate and ever
and the only if that matters.

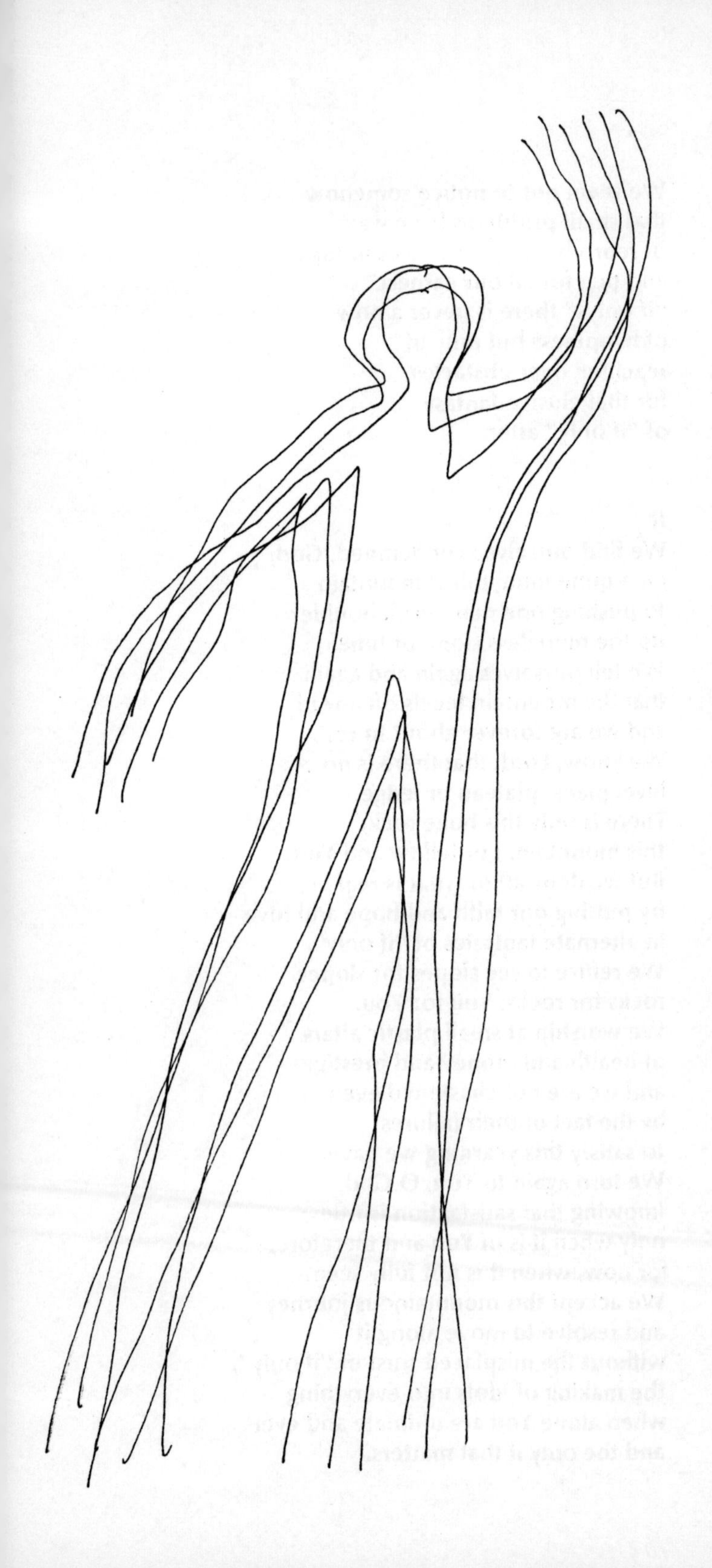

"The Spirit himself intercedes
for us with sighs too deep for words."

Romans 8,27

If the still-points
of our turning worlds
are cores of chaos,
unresolved tensions,
bundles of conflict,
angers with God
for calling us to this
how can we pray?
We shake our fists
at you, Lord of Chaos.
We cling to this,
that you are breathing
your Spirit into us,
into our struggles
for some integrity.
Our sufferings,
stammerings, even
our mad mutterings
will be real prayer
if your Spirit breathes.

The good news we hear
is that you and he
begin and complete it all,
the talking, listening,
even our answering back.
If we are bold
it is because all words
fail, ideas collapse,
structures burn down
and there is left
nothing but a violence
about our need for you.

"Consumatum est"

John 19,30

**Thread-shed and shivering
at cold of strange new sheets,
at first-time fears
of being still alone.
Two movings together
and wantings to help,
two slow naked nudgings
onto, under and in.
One fast growing flesh,
one pulse pounding
basic beats of blood,
one both-borrowed body.
A faint flash of sharing,
two sights of a self,
two deaths well done
for one now being born.**

II
**God become man for mocking,
warm Sonship unrobed,
stripped for the chilling**

of fear found strange.
His wild wooing of men,
a laying down in dirt
and being lifted up
against the maiden sky.
Flesh in shreds instead
of words unheard, unsaid.
The pain pounded
an arch into His back.
An ecstacy of joining
as before, but now as man,
and sealing death well done,
the Spirit now being born.

"Woe to those so snug
. . . the revelry is over."

Amos 6,1 & 7

This still young world of ours
is taking on the ancient look
of starvation-dead babies.
Famine has become the only
affirmation for too many,
food the only meaning;
there are mouths eating
in too many dreams,
in too few homes.
Waste is at work in bodies.
Withering is a world-wide pastime.
Hunger is a lengthening shadow
arching from China, over India,
cutting through holy lands
to European cities and valleys
of, even, Mississippi USA.
Two of us out of three
stand with empty hands,
palms turned please and up.

They go sadly, with faces
long and desperate for their children.
They quaver for a crumb.

II

We are judged by hunger now,
we who adorn ourselves, doing well,
who feed more by far
to our dogs and precious cats
than to those shadowed men
whose bones are numbered,
whose sides are pierced
by what we throw away.
God, help us who have this dreaded
power to feed every of your sons.
Help us in our affluence
to, in fact, begin to do so.
And, God, help those especially
whose desperation makes them
wait, starving, for us
to see through their silence,
to move through this marsh
of our own damned indifference.

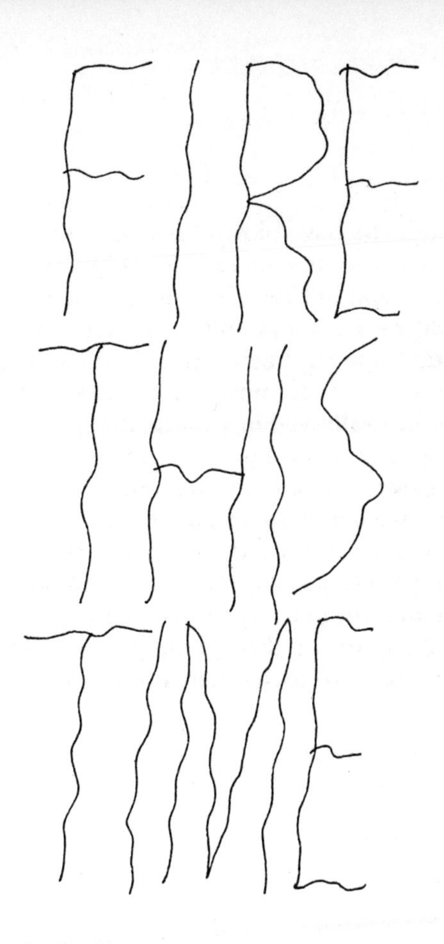

"Violence will no longer
be heard of in your country"

Isaiah 60,18

Oh, the stoning, frenzied, at-arms
smell of each of us these days.
Every gate to every city is posted,
children play at peace-games now.
We are going quickly rigid with fear,
all of us, each has his enemy there.
We run at night down open roads,
at day through hidden arches of our hope,
but out of every silence threats of fire
stop us, make us turn and stare
until we no longer can deny that
a mass of wild-eyed strangers, us, lives
where we in honey-days grew young,
that silence itself has become more
than shrill trumpet blast and moan enough.

II

God, you have blown life into ashes,
we believe it, courage into cold.
We stand between lines in iron drawn
and we for our people, our selves are afraid.
Our hope has been caught in some threat
and we wonder now if it has finally
been swallowed in a subtle draught of hopelessness.
We have, God, a promise from you,
elusive, difficult, not quite fickle,
and we dare now recall you to it.
We do, but still and with an effort always,
on your terms, your hidden hellish terms.
Be present to us, your violent people
looking to you through flames real and coming.
Be peace for us, a quenching ocean of it.

"Then the eyes of both of them
were opened and they realized that
they were naked."

Genesis 3,7

A man and this woman
hover together near an edge
electric, hungry, still and ready
over their quilted twilight selves.
This was the scene, green with passion,
deep with rivers after rain unknown,
a pool of images, wet and yearning,
a man and this woman.
They do not touch, but only thirst
in their dry and hesitant flesh.
The man leans a calculated measure
to prod the images of the pool
closer, closer, perhaps into one.
Veins, of water or of blood,
of a man or of this woman,
gather into thunder and pound,
making a quiver and more of their hovering,
building passion, power and hope.
They see from their leaning edge

the gentle crossing of her face by his
but instead of the one true kiss,
it is a first and final eclipse in the pool
of her longing face by his.
The still hovering in hope was broken
and when he turned, stunned
to the full face of her flesh
he saw cowered in those eyes in shame
a man, no woman and tears.

II

God, who has done this to us?
Why is one true kiss impossible?
Or, at best, so fast and gone?
We are trapped in deepness, in cold,
and consistent tenderness eludes us.
There are, we have tasted, times
when hoverings are together and red
with passion pure and quick and sure.
But we fumble them away, never worthy
afterwards of union worth the name.
God, we, men and women, all and all
eclipse each other bloodily to death.
Take our longing. Make it for You,
because alone we are too brutal.
Be gentle with us and in such a way
that we, poor naked ones, might learn.

"The Lord secures justice and the rights of all the oppressed."

Psalm 102,6

O, Lord, why did you make this world so big?
Only giants could live here rightly,
and we are not giants
but only a people of common size.
We are deathly afraid, Lord,
for everywhere there are powers
of oppression and hunger and war;
We are deathly afraid, Lord,
for we are clothed in those powers
ourselves; we are oppressors.
Yet we would be otherwise.
We would have justice for all,
for our own poor and others.
We would have ample food
for everyman and opportunity,
the food of every human spirit.
We know that we must love
each other or die.
Yet we are in business as usual,
pushing our boulders uphill,

pursuing all kinds of small 'g' gods.
We know it, Lord, as a people
that we are by indifference, default,
a race of oppressors, slayers perhaps.
We would like to be a flame
of hope, affirmation, justice.
But we too are victims,
we too are oppressed, slayed men.
We are beaten by ourselves and
some nameless thing more and,
as we say, we are not giants.
So everyone suffers, though we, perhaps, less.
We rise for this moment at least
above the obscuring dust and smoke
of our busy-ness to You.
We hand this worry for the
course of our world
over to You, God, our Father,
for you have promised
to secure justice for the oppressed.
You are the only giant, God.
We men of common size
accept responsibility for this
world and all its victims,
but we do so, we will try,
only because we believe your Word
that justice is your Work
and that in your strength,
through our common weakness
we can do better, perhaps best.

"I have made you a light
for the nations, so that
my salvation may reach the
ends of the earth."

Acts 13,47

Look down, look down
with mercy-healing, Lord.
Your light is shaken,
the Pope has spoken,
this church is broken.
Bishops ask obedience,
parish priests wonder.
Most marrieds of us
shrug off the word
of hard authority.
Many move away
reluctantly from us.
Others simply suffer.
And we wonder why
in this broken world
your people must tear
at each others' lives,
why this broken world

is broken yet more
by your broken church.
The question puts itself
squarely to our faith
in your promise to care
with love's hovering for us;
can you use us, pope
bishops, priests, all,
human as we are,
to bring yet some light
to this dark world,
some hope to this torn,
human as it ever is?
When there are wars
and mere rumors of peace,
why are we yet more?
Can you use us,
small-minded, hating,
to bring abundant life?
Or shall we now die
in this committee
of pope, bishops, priests
and every one of us?
If life came from death,
if wholeness sprouted
out of all brokenness,
if what your son said
is true and present,
then this broken world
may yet be stunned
into one, into you,
by this broken, crying
fallen-down sign lifted-up,
your gathered church,
your problem people.
Make it so, Lord.
Make it so.

"And that's the way it is."
Walter said before someone sang
that bufferins are better
than last year's model.
We settle back to relax
to be massaged into
believing that wives indeed
are beautiful at breakfast
and enemies have names
that tell you who they are.
Their strength outlasts
a commercial or two
but the triumph of good
is a sixty-minute matter
of laughter and gadgets
and some babe's smile.
When evening is as old as dozes
and the set is most succeeding,
when we are become our chairs
and things for once are clear
and simple and understandable,
some late-night walter intrudes
and tries to break the spell,
tries to say with color film

that none of prime time is true;
"That's not the way it is."
Housewives are not only ugly
at breakfast; they have bad breath.
There are not only wild ways to live
but wild ways to die;
500 men each week by Cong,
occassional hippies by shooting speed.
There is no news but bad news
and we prefer (understandably)
the machied paper of prime time.

II

O Lord, forgive us television,
what we do with it and within it.
We hide in numb fantasy,
frightened yet caught by cool
Conkritish pessimisms, pains.
We forget the only living color
that is wing-spread all the time,
the smashing red of your son
and his good news, extra,
live, every day and night
until the late late show
of his coming again in person,
alive, prime of time and the end.

"Eye has not seen what things God"
1 Corinthians 2,9

I have a hardest saying to say you softly.
Be credulous in listening if you can.
If not, then listen at least, linger
times out of testing the bubbles
and boulevards of your expectancy.
What I have to say is what I saw again
low in the sky, low beneath huckleberries
on the horizon under a bush where I lay.
I saw it, hard as any twig, clear
as the star that twitters mornings
through embracing mists of dew.
Pure as any bell it rang.
Listen, I saw, heard, felt, tasted
cried for someone to come and see.
Be there with me now under a bush
lower than spider webs
wet with night's quick get-away.
Hear what soft I saw, eyes closed.
See what hard I say;
one clear quick of eternity.

II

**God, I'm seeing things,
spots of you before my eyes,
lots of new patterns purple
in kaleidoscopes of quick interiority.
Where light comes from when dark
and tight with pain my lids
are lashed together closed
I do not know or think to care.
But seeing things low under bushes
can be surprise after eyes seal off
supposedly sight and light.
Where dark should biologically have been
these lots of new spots of You,
all the old images out of childhood,
all the new futures out of age
dance a morning rosy round
and gift me gently into smiles.**

" 'My people', says the Lord,
'shall be filled with my good things' "
Jeremiah 31,14

We give you thanks, O God, for orange juice,
for chevrolets, for grandchildren in the sun,
for mere glances between daughters and men,
for a thousand amber miles of summertime.
We give you thanks for these six tall feet,
for seventy years, for that nameless center
that points us toy-boat-like to You.
We give you thanks, O God, for mud pies
and for the great delight of sharing them,
of showing them to passing strangers,
for the joy of confiding our mud together.
We give you thanks for carter's ink
and all the easy things we daily use
and never think about or notice.
We thank you for the alphabet and most
especially for the marvelous letter 'Z'
which, like ourselves, looks so pointed
and painful, but given chance to show itself
is easy, soft, lazy, slightly secret.
We thank you for the many beautiful arms

about us and our village, the world.
We thank you, O God, for Christ who died
on our village cross, our own, for us,
who wept in the ruins of our winter,
whose bloody tears have fallen on tombs
meant for grandchildren in the sun,
for daughters and men, for passing strangers;
whose bloody tears gather in everlasting pools
of goodness under breath, over death.
We celebrate Christ with orange juice
and our conscientious happy mud pies,
and with the beautiful arms of sound
that His letter 'Z' still makes as we
thank you, O God, who fill us with Him.

Church basements
were never clean
and till these Council
years never seen.
Now, beneath statues
and candles while they last
new choirs of Sunday singers
prepare the music mass.
So we gathered, the girls
and we few men,
"to lead", they said, but
none said how or when.
The common goal was to
use your voice the least;
timids shared by all
were hoarded by the priest.
We who started by standing
soon found a seat and sat.
By then some tempers,
as well as notes, were flat.
Someone muttered close to me
"Let's finish, God above!"
Just one more song, they said,
a thing called "God is love".

We sang. "The love of
Christ has gathered us . . ."
But then the leader
started to fuss;
"Dammit that note
goes up half a notch!"
The guy next to me
looked at his watch.
We sang, "By this
shall all know . . ."
And two or three
got up to go.
Two chairs over a
lady sucked her pen.
When I looked up later
there were no other men.
We sang, "We are all
partakers of the one Bread."
I wanted to kick
someone in the head.
Last verse done
we rushed to repeat
"God is love", but
we'd lost the beat.
We meet again Sunday,
for its we who lead.
Thank God its God
who does the Deed.

"Though it seemed Abraham's hope
could not be fulfilled
he hoped and he believed."

Romans 4,18

If, indeed, the day before days began
there was a hovering over chaos
with its dirty waters and baffled dark,
can time or its torment deny us?
If a bird could hang forever in the air
above its craning young in some nest,
warming, wings weary, the currents they breathe,
who can suffocate alone or freeze?
If dust, particles of pebbles, was scooped once
gently into a pile of certain special shape
and given then such a set of nostrils
that could take a kiss of breath and breathe,
if dust could grow a rib and lose it
and bear no scar but the light one of love,
if none could be one, then two for three,
perhaps an image is saying us someone.
If from a hill or tree in some once oasis
the far-circle horizon seemed walkable,
the edge of possession close enough to seize,
our leaving for the desert may be understood.

If, indeed, when we were last past cursing
and thirst had killed even our crawl,
the eastern horizon did uplift itself and come
to us with water and a single word of love,
if it was no mirage, though who's to say,
and unreachable beyond went beyond itself
to come where the compass crossed in us,
then it may be the edge of our there is here.
If, strange thought, all this is so,
mystery may dawn the clear mastery of dusk
and the pattern perhaps of these 'ifs' will show
that even our blind guess is guise of God.

*"How long before he dies
and his name perishes?"*

Psalm 41,5

**A man sat waiting by an old woods path
piled high by then by leaves of many falls.
Quick sylvan things played hide and seek with sounds
where men had made a slash between the trees,
a wound that opened thinly on the sky.
The going way of man, the thickening years
has scabbed the path, a faint and hidden scar.
It was forgotten then by birds and squirrels,
by all except a small, half-crumbled wall
that didn't seem to know the trail was gone
or that the ditch it guarded had been filled in;
by all except the man who'd come to wait,
to watch the path and lean against its wall.
The man was waiting for the thickening
of sky, the opening up of time's old wound,
was waiting for the thinning out of trees.
A leaf, dead, zig-zagged to rest upon his leg.**

II

**God, death makes life itself a slow disease.
We are the world's cry against time's old wound,
and You are, O God to whom we cling, ours.
Our cry against death is not a phrase,**

not a curse to darkness, no argument.
Our cry against is in a single breathing out,
in an exercise of muscles, lung tissue and air.
We, saying no, have become time's moan,
and You, saying yes, have become ours.
Save us from death, the thickening of sky.
Spare us the deaths of now, enliven us.
Listen, God, to our breathing in and out,
hear it, our nearest thing to eloquence,
and make us somehow someday ever live.

"What we call the beginning
is often the end and to make an end
is to make a beginning.
The end is where we start from."

T. S. Eliot

So it is with buds and birds and babies grown old,
with grey-haired men whose pants are rolled
in neat little cuffs sharp as any boy's.
But when ends for friends bewitch beginnings
silence is noise.
The end is in theory as good a place as any
to start from once again, provided the many
moments of being-in-between were neutral things.
But what if they were hammers kissing the bell
to rings?
Every end, no matter how described or felt, is part
of death.
The end that rends the ringing surrounds the breath
of bell-like men as if all air was a plastic laundry bag.
Dying is the choking of lungs, turning of tongues
to rag.

II

God, with ended rags You have begun the widest
of good news.
Such is Your season of cycles in which winners lose
that every A is somehow Z, every You is maybe me

and the leavings off of one is falling leaf of we.
Things come, as You say, in circles, as so perhaps
they go.
When Your finish, the final one, has coaxed from
the world its Oh,
it will be seen that only one thing ended the first
time round,
only one thing truly began when losers-weepers
were finally found.
Into our circle of cycling so and search You have
poured
all beginnings and every end, Yourself, as You said,
Our Lord.
Death itself has been differented to life, the circle
is complete
with Your cup-shaped promise to every tender
thing repeat.

"In your way lies joy beyond all wealth."
Psalm 119,14

**Shall we a moment pause the practised pessimism
that underwrites our time of two wars,
our harvest of worry over peace and no peace?
When flames lick at Washington and Sioux City
and when, in short order, Kennedys bleed away
and poor blacks bleed but never quite away
or red enough on television to be noticed,
when, in a word, we are overcome nearly
by killing crisis after searing crisis,
the oldest and always newest joys are lost.
We need times to raise them up again;
a child, think of it, just did his first
bit of catching at breath, is screaming
out the ecstacy of life as a man.
Streets are full of ball-throwing boys,
and the window just hit doesn't break at all.
Wives and husbands after anger are apologizing;
there will be roses and fine cooking tonight.
An anonymous alcoholic trying so hard
will sleep again with still thirsty victory
and there will be smiles on the slumber**

of his son, his daughter, his trying wife.
A little boy has just tied his first shoe.
Teenagers here and there are full of respect,
and parents here and there are reasonable.
Another plane has landed safe, nearly on time.
And a galaxy of muscles are stretched
in the catching, joyous smile of now.

II

God, in our worried hearts we hide often from you
and from each other in old anxieties.
We forget that smiles at all the simple joys
are the surest signs of your being here.
You have given us a world full of children
and a night-time full of laughing stars.
The message is so simple we may miss it;
You are here in all of our everything:
in relief at windows hit and still unbroken,
in arguments ended at last in embracing,
in happy shocks of understanding between men.
Remind us, Lord, with strange seizures of joy
that these hates and wars and widowed hearts,
these moans of our time are exceptional.
Remind us, Lord, with ordinary happiness
that You have overcome all worlds of grief
and even now are wrapping us in coats
of common daily happenings of goodness.
Strip us, Lord, of melancholy strangeness,
for we accept your word, not that misery
is unreal or painless, but that all of life
is quick, shot through with You and therefore,
fundamentally, with miles and smiles of joy.

"Only a little while now,
a very little while . . ."

Hebrews 10,37

It feels like meanwhile all the time,
this heavy mean between long ago and someday.
Time moves like a cripple through a crowd,
everybody watching and waiting to go on,
to get on, get out, get going again at last.
We started by waiting out some definite,
the world or we to come finally of age,
better weather, the next election.
Or for some of us, the start was waiting
with held breath for this certain second coming.
For others, it has been for a first forever.
Now we wait, each one, for waiting's sake
and every cry is captive, eyesight routine,
deepest down things postponed indefinitely.
Words like "when" or "then" slipped unseen
out of every but vaguest meaning.
We have become a clock-collecting people,
yet have lost in dumb faces the face we seek.
Time, having lost as well its legs, limps,

never gets by or goes easily or unnoticed.
We can hear it crawl among the leaves
and sunlight in its fading is a noise.

II

God, we say that we wait You out,
wait to see with our unhidden eyes
that all we say that you say is indeed
true and You and the bursting out
of Your Son at the end at last.
We ask, certainly, that our waiting
through these meanwhiles be worth it.
But more, we need some worth-it now,
some present soil of significance
to curl our toes in, to plant a rose in.
We work at waiting without idols,
but slip easily into waiting without You.
Be with us quickening and real
now, when we believe, then when we are bored.

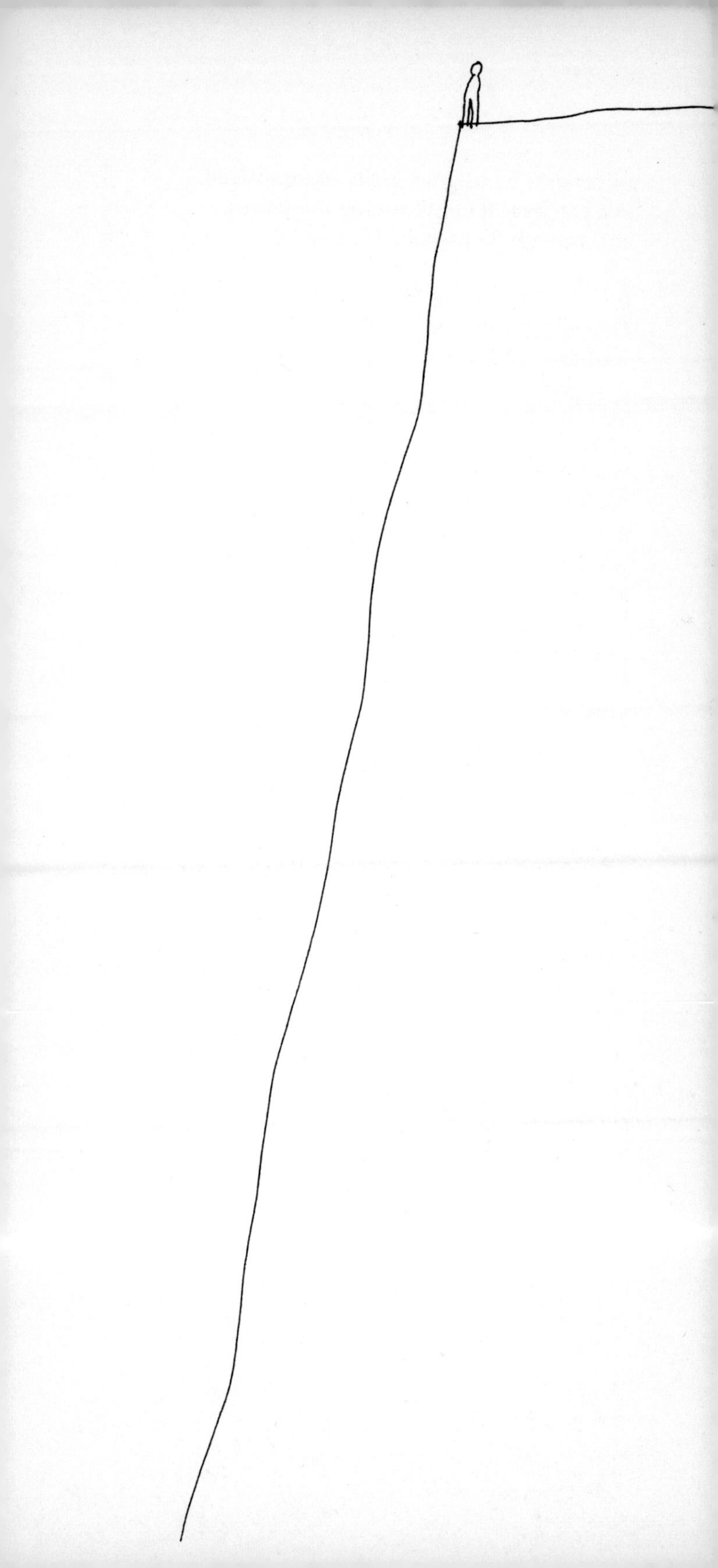